Library of Congress Control Number:2019909095

Kids Can Change the World

Young Readers' Edition

Adom Appiah

Dear Reader,
The purpose of this book is to inspire
and motivate kids to do their best.

Your friend,
Adom

What do you want to do when you grow up?

You don't have to wait to grow up to do great things. You can start now.

Do you have an idea today?

Together, we can make a difference.

Are you ready?

Let's go!

Remember to have fun and do your best!

Don't forget to write down the steps
that make your idea work.

Sometimes, it is good to ask for advice from others. They may help make your idea better!

Don't worry if you fail. You can always
learn from the process and bounce back!

When your idea grows into a
project, tell people about
it so they can support your work!

Hurray! Your idea worked.
This is your time to shine! Be proud!

Mission accomplished! Take time to rest
and think back on your adventure.

Always work hard and dream big!
The world is yours!

We can change the world! Let's go!!

OTHER BOOKS BY ADOM APPIAH

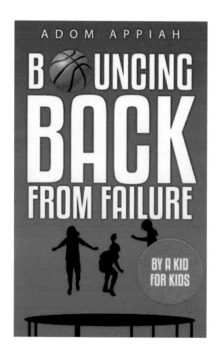

Made in the USA
Monee, IL
19 February 2020